When KIDDY Was Home Alone

When Kiddy was Home Alone

ISBN: 978-1-990380-18-1
9 781990 380181

Book Design by Roberta Chang
Guava Press™ is a Trademark of Blue Tang Ltd.
Guava Press, Blue Tang Ltd., Newmarket, ON L3X 2R6, Canada
ISBN 978-1-990380-18-1
Printed in India

When KIDDY Was Home Alone

Written by **Al Campbell**
Illustrated by **Roberta Chang**

This is the story of when Kiddy was home alone.
On that fateful day the goat wandered and roamed.

Kiddy entered the kitchen looking for breakfast;
She was hungry for a bellyful to all day long last.

Kiddy saw on the countertop a carton of eggs;
She-goat reached for the box but it fell on her head.

All the eggs broke, no more and no less;
The kitchen floor became a total mess.

Kiddy licked up the broken eggs all over the floor;
Her tummy wasn't full so she wandered some more.

In the dining room Kiddy saw a huge loaf of bread.
She knew it was fresh and wouldn't fall on her head.

Kiddy bit into the bread like she hadn't been fed;
And in a minute she was stuffed and ready for bed.

She went to the bedroom where a mirror stood tall;
And admired her beauty as she leant against a wall.

Kiddy soon saw a dress sticking out of the closet;
So she put on the frock, as well as a blue bonnet.

Kiddy also put on eye shadow, rouge and lipstick;
And polished her hooves to look like red bricks.

Kiddy danced to the tune of her own secret drum;
And soon the goat felt dizzy as if she drank rum.

Kiddy fell on the bed with a pillow under her head;
She snuggled a blanket and laid there half-dead.

Kiddy slept for a short while, it was only a nap;
When she awoke there was drool down to her lap.

Kiddy wanted to be fresh so she went to the bath;
The nanny filled it with water and then added salt.

She washed her body with soap and shampoo too;
There was no beauty treatment the goat didn't do.

Kiddy leaped from the bath still soaking wet;
And strutted to the living room like an indoor pet.

Kiddy lounged on the sofa like a true couch potato;
And hummed a sweet tune while eating a tomato.

After finishing the tomato she pranced outside;
Stood on the verandah and rubbed her backside.

That was when Kiddy saw a bird on the lawn;
It looked tastier than all the food eaten since dawn.

Kiddy ran to the lawn and snapped at the bird;
She slipped and did fall, and then span in a whirl.

Kiddy slid on her back all the way to a flowerbed;
And there she did stop after banging her head.

Kiddy lay among the flowers that were once so tall;
Her head did hurt for she had hit it against a wall.

Kiddy moaned and groaned like a wounded nanny;
There she did lie more helpless than an old granny.

When young Boysie came back from the tuck shop,
He heard moaning and groaning so he had to stop.

Boysie saw that Kiddy had caused a huge mess;
And knew his mother would have lots of distress.

The boy dragged the she-goat out of the flowerbed;
Many plants were damaged and some even dead.

Boysie struggled to pull little Kiddy to the backyard;
She put up lots of resistance; it was extremely hard.

Finally, Boysie yanked Kiddy into the goat pen,
And said, "You must never come out ever again!"

As the little boy walked away he mumbled to himself,
"What sweet nanny goat will run her belly!"
Meaning: What seems nice now, might not be so later.